# Peacemaker

## and Other Stories

Stories by
Malorie Blackman, Nicholas Fisk,
David Belbin and Tony Bradman

Illustrated by
Peter Richardson and David Hine

# Contents

# Peacemaker

*Malorie Blackman*

'Michela Corbin, what did I just say?'

The class began to snigger. I looked up,
dismayed. There, right in front of my desk,
stood Teacher Faber. I hadn't seen her
coming! I tried to cover my literature
screen with my hand but the teacher was
too quick for me. She snatched up my
screen and started to read the story I'd
been writing.

'Michela Corbin, you are supposed to be writing an essay on Section 415 of the Peace Treaty between the Alliance and the Inthral Sector. Not this...this...this!'

'I'm sorry. I'll erase it.' I grabbed for my screen. Teacher Faber snatched it back.

'Let us take a look at what has so captured your attention,' said the teacher sarcastically. '...I spun around, quick as a Pogett snake. Davin lunged at me with her laz-sword. Immediately I swung my weapon down to parry her thrust. The sound of laser beam on laser beam zinged almost musically. With a furious roar, Davin whipped her laz-sword upwards towards my head. I ducked and stepped back simultaneously. I didn't want to hurt her but one touch from the laz-sword was lethal – and I wasn't about to die. I...' Teacher Faber stopped reading, but not before my face was on fire.

'This tish-tosh is dangerous nonsense. I told you the last time that you'd had your final warning. Now you'll go on report – again!' said Teacher Faber with satisfaction. 'And I shall make sure that your mother sees this...this story of yours.'

My blood ran icy cold. 'My mother will go nuts! I'll do the essay. I'll stay behind and work late. Oh please, you can't…'

'Watch me,' said Teacher Faber. 'I don't know what's wrong with you, Michela. You persist with writing these kinds of stories.'

'They're adventure stories,' I protested. 'They're just fiction.'

'You humans are supposed to abhor violence of any kind – even in stories,' said Teacher Faber. 'And yet, Michela, you insist on reading forbidden books like *Treasure Island* and *The Three Musketeers*, and on writing this kind of fantastical, dangerous foolishness.'

It wasn't my fault I read forbidden books. If they weren't forbidden in the first place, then I wouldn't get into trouble for reading them! Mother owned an impressive collection of nineteenth and twentieth-century fiction books, most of them now classified as forbidden. I'd been caught with Mother's books more than once and Mother threatened to burn them all if I was caught with just one of them again. So instead of reading them, I'd taken to writing my own – but that seemed to get me into even worse trouble!

'I won't read or write any more,' I pleaded. 'Please don't report me.'

Teacher Faber keyed in some commands on the console that was situated on her stomach.

'It is done.' Teacher Faber moved away. 'A full report has been transmitted to your mother.'

I scowled at her. Rotten, Pogett-brained, Valunian weasel! I groaned. What was my mother going to say?

'Teacher Faber sent me yet another demerit report on you today.'

'Mother, I can explain...'

Mother flopped down into her favourite recliner and kicked off her shoes. 'Michela, I don't want to hear it,' she sighed. 'I've reasoned with you, pleaded with you, argued until I'm blue.'

'It was only a story, Mother,' I said quietly.

'A story! Why can't you write stories about proper subjects? What's wrong with peace and diplomacy and friendship? Why must you revel in violence?'

'I don't,' I said furiously. 'They're only stories, Mother...'

'They're a way of thinking. They're a way of being,' my mother replied. 'You persist in embarrassing me in front of my colleagues. Think of what your father would say if he was still alive.'

And with that one single argument, Mother forced me to shut up and not argue.

An uncomfortable silence filled the room.

'Michela, have you been recoding your Peacemaker?'

'Of course not!' I blustered.

After the 'Treasure Island' incident, I'd been sent to Doctor Bevan to have my Peacemaker checked out. Everyone had a Peacemaker permanently attached to the inside of their left wrist on their eleventh birthday. The Peacemaker was a small, grey disk which looked like one of those old-fashioned buttons people used to use to fasten their clothes. Doctor Bevan explained that it was a behavioural inhibitor – supposed to ensure that the non-aggression we'd all been taught for the last century was more than just a lesson. The Peacemaker was supposed to make sure that it was physically impossible for us humans to be aggressive. No more wars, no more fights, we couldn't hurt each other any more.

Only it didn't stop there. Books and films that had once been considered classics had now been banned. And more and more things these days were taken as signs of belligerence, like talking, laughing and singing too loudly – and as I do all three, I'm constantly on report!

And that was the problem really. I was always letting Mother down – and we both knew it.

Mother shook her head sadly. 'Why do you do it? I read your story, Michela. Is that really what's in your head – in spite of everything I've tried to teach you?'

'It was just a story, Mother,' I whispered unhappily.

'And the part where you were fighting with the laz-sword?' Mother asked.

'I put that in because it's the only weapon I've seen a hologram of,' I said.

'You told me that you wanted to train in Je-kan-ia for the exercise, to teach you balance and co-ordination. It's obvious what's in your mind as you use the Kan-ia – you pretend it's a real weapon instead of the plastic stick it is. I forbid you to practise that so-called sport in the future,' said Mother.

'But it's the only thing I'm any good at,' I protested. Don't take that away from me. Not that as well, I thought desperately. But from the look on Mother's face, I knew she really meant it.

'And you can go to Doctor Bevan right this minute and get your Peacemaker checked out. And if you have been tampering with it…'

'CON ONE! CON ONE! Captain

Corbin to the bridge immediately. Captain Corbin to the bridge.'

Mother was interrupted in mid-sentence. She slipped her shoes back on to her feet and within seconds she was out the door. I stared after her. What was going on? What had happened to take us from Condition Four – our usual state – to Condition One, which was only used for extreme, imminent danger?

I was used to Mother, as captain of the ship, being called away at a moment's notice. At first it'd seemed exciting to have such an important mother – captain of the *Kitabu*, one of the most prestigious ships in the Alliance fleet. Recently the excitement had faded away to leave something else, something less noble, in its place. I hardly ever saw her. And it seemed to me that Mother was always Captain Corbin first and being my mother came a long way down the list. I didn't want to feel the way I did, but I couldn't help it.

'Come on, Michela,' I muttered, trying to pull myself together. What should I do now? I glanced down at my Peacemaker. Whatever the emergency was, it'd saved me from getting into real trouble.

There was only one way to find out what was going on. I left the room and headed up to the bridge. Maybe I could sneak in without Mother seeing me.

But the moment I stepped on to the bridge, I gasped, then froze. There, directly in front of the *Kitabu* was the biggest ship I'd ever seen. Only a small portion of it filled the entire viewscreen. It must have had some kind of sensor-jamming device to appear before us like this without any warning.

There was no way anyone would throw me off the bridge. All eyes were on the colossal ship before us.

'Ensign Natsua, activate the universal decoder. Open a channel,' Mother said. She was sitting before the viewer on the bridge, her face solemn. 'This is Captain Corbin of the Alliance ship, *Kitabu*. We come in peace. Our mission is to negotiate trade and route lines through this sector. Do you understand?'

Each encounter with a new alien species called for Mother to issue a similar blurb. The idea was that the alien ship would analyse the words spoken, so that any further communication to them could be translated. That's the way our universal decoder worked as well.

After only a few moments, the face and upper body of one of the alien crew appeared on the viewer. And such a face as

I'd never seen before. My breath caught in my throat and refused to budge. The alien's face held only one eye in what was presumably its forehead. Its nose dominated its face, moving in a series of ridges downwards and outwards. It had lips – different from humans but similar enough to be recognizable as such. But the thing that made me stare without blinking and turned my stomach over was the alien's skin. It was transparent. I could see grey liquid running through tiny canals in its body. I could see the tops of two organs, one on either side of its upper body, contracting and expanding. The two organs had to be the alien's hearts. The whole thing looked strange, bizarre – and totally disgusting!

'This is Captain Corbin of the Alliance ship, *Kitabu*. We come in peace. Do you understand?' Mother repeated.

'I am Fflqa-Tur, a Chamrah knight. And I understand perfectly,' the alien replied. 'You have entered our sector without permission and must pay the price.'

'The price?' Mother questioned sharply.

'Our ships are now at war,' said Fflqa-Tur.

'We were not aware that permission was required. My ship is the first Alliance ship to enter this sector. We in the Alliance are peaceful, non-confrontational. We meant no harm.'

'Harm or not, it is Chamrah law. We are now at war.'

'We will not fight you.'

'You have no choice,' said the alien.

'We are prepared to leave this sector and never return,' said Mother.

'You cannot retreat,' Fflqa-Tur said. 'Your path lies ahead.'

Silence.

'Comms down,' Mother instructed the ensign. That way she could hear what Fflqa-Tur had to say but not vice versa. 'Lieutenant Dopp, what's the maximum speed of Fflqa-Tur's vessel?'

'Vel Five, according to our sensors,' the navigation officer replied.

'Comms up,' Mother ordered, to resume two-way communication. 'Fflqa-Tur, I must repeat, we in the Alliance are peace-loving. We will not fight with you. Our ship can travel at more than twice the speed of your craft. I am prepared to use that speed to withdraw so that our meeting does not end in violence.'

'Run if you must,' said Fflqa-Tur. 'But I will spend the rest of my days searching for you throughout the galaxy. The challenge has been issued. It is not yours to reject.'

'But this makes no sense. Why won't you let us leave? Why must we fight?' Mother asked, an edge creeping into her voice.

'It is our way. And if you leave, not only will our two ships be at war, but my people on Chamrah will be at war with your so-called Alliance,' said Fflqa-Tur. There was a pause before he added, 'I am also bound to inform you of an alternative option, as you did not deliberately break our laws.'

'I'm listening,' Mother said eagerly.

'You may send over your champion to fight against the best knight on my ship,' said Fflqa-Tur.

Mother's shoulders slumped momentarily. 'We have many champions – but not of fighting. Never of fighting.'

'Then how do you propose that we proceed with our combat?' asked Fflqa-Tur.

'As far as I'm concerned, we don't proceed at all. No one on this ship will fight you. It's against everything we believe in.'

Mother began to finger the necklace that Father had given her years before. It was her only sign of nervousness. I could almost hear her thinking, her expression was so intent. 'I have an alternative of my own to suggest.'

'Proceed,' the alien barked.

'We surrender,' Mother said, seriously.

No one on the bridge moved. Fflqa-Tur's expression was as unreadable and as immovable as an Earth monolith. He beckoned to one of his own bridge crew, and they whispered together for a few moments.

Fflqa-Tur turned back to the viewer. 'We are unfamiliar with the word "surrender". Explain.'

'It means we concede defeat, we submit, we yield. We will give ourselves over to you,' Mother said. 'We will not fight.'

Fflqa-Tur smiled. 'Your Alliance is worthless. A Chamrah baby has more courage, more valour. You will stand and fight. Or you will stand and die. The choice is yours. You have fifty locshans to prepare.'

Fflqa-Tur's image disappeared from the viewer to be replaced by his ship.

'Locshans?' asked Mother.

'A moment, Captain,' said Lieutenant Dopp. Silence reigned for several seconds as the lieutenant manually keyed into the universal decoder. 'Fifty locshans would appear to be the equivalent of ten Earth minutes.'

'Ensign, open another channel. I've got to try and reason with them,' said Mother after a pause.

'They're not responding, Captain,' said the ensign.

'Keep trying.' Mother went back to her seat.

'What do we do, Captain?' asked the ensign.

'If they don't answer…we prepare to die,' Mother said, still staring at the viewer. 'We will not endanger the Alliance. We will not fight.'

'We could leave this sector,' suggested the ensign.

'No. We're not going to run,' said Mother. 'I'm not going to let this escalate into a full-blown war between the Alliance and the Chamrah nation. We must try to get through to them, but if not…'

Mother didn't say any more, she didn't have to.

I stared at her. Would she really let us all die, without even a fight? Looking around the bridge, everyone wore the same expression as Mother on their faces. I had my answer.

I looked down at my Peacemaker. How I wished I hadn't tampered with it. The others on the bridge were obviously prepared to do as Mother had said and die rather than go against their beliefs. Me? I wanted to fight. And the feeling was so strong that it scared me. What could I do? I was only thirteen.

'Mother, can I…?' I began.

Mother's head whipped around. 'Michela, get off the bridge. You're not supposed to be up here.' She didn't even let me finish.

I looked at her. She looked at me, worry and resignation on her face. And at that moment, I knew it was hopeless. We were going to die. I turned away. Unexpectedly, Mother called me back and hugged me.

'Go to our quarters,' Mother said gently. 'I'll join you later.'

After a pause, I left the bridge without another word – but it wasn't to go back to our quarters. It was too late to wonder what I would've done and how I would've felt if I hadn't tampered with my Peacemaker. The point was, I had. And if Fflqa-Tur of the Chamrah wanted a fighter, he would get one.

'Shuttle pod three, you are ordered to identify yourself.' My mother's voice echoed all around the small shuttle pod.

I didn't answer. I couldn't answer – not yet. Not until I had finished rejigging the remote control codes and the forcefield cycle. Once that was done, I opened a channel to the alien ship.

'This is shuttle pod three. I wish to speak to Fflqa-Tur.' I kept repeating the message.

'Michela? What do you think you're doing?' Mother's face appeared on the shuttle pod viewer to my right. Her expression was incredulous, her voice furious. 'Michela, bring that shuttle pod back to this ship at once.'

'I can't, Mother. Please don't try to stop me,' I said.

'Ensign Natsua, lock on to that shuttle pod and bring it back,' Mother commanded.

'I can't, Captain. The remote control codes have been changed. We can no longer control that pod,' the ensign replied.

'Then use the tractor beam to bring her back,' Mother snapped.

'Sorry, Captain,' the ensign replied after a few moments. 'The pod's forcefield frequency has been recalibrated. I can't get a lock.'

'Michela, bring that pod back now and I promise we'll say no more about it. Running away from this ship isn't the answer. Your pod can't outrun the Chamrah. Your place is on this ship – no matter what happens,' said Mother.

I stared at her. I couldn't believe it. Did she really think I was trying to run away, to escape the *Kitabu's* inevitable fate? Is that what she really thought of me?

'Bye, Mother,' I said quietly, and I switched off the viewer. I carried on sending out my hailing message to Fflqa-Tur.

Without warning his image appeared on my viewer. I swallowed hard.

'Fflqa-Tur.' I coughed to clear my throat. 'Fflqa-Tur, I am Michela Corbin of the Alliance ship, *Kitabu*. I have come to accept your challenge.'

Fflqa-Tur's eye narrowed, 'You are a human?'

'Yes.'

'You are a knight?'

'Not as such.'

'You are a warrior.'

'Not quite. But it doesn't matter what I am. I'm accepting your challenge,' I said.

There was a deathly hush. Then came a moment when every part of me, every drop of blood in my body, froze, as if I had been suddenly plunged into a bath of liquid nitrogen. The next thing I knew I was standing directly in front of Fflqa-Tur.

'W-what happened?' I whispered.

Fflqa-Tur spoke to me but I didn't understand. I shook my head. Someone behind him came up to me and injected something into my ear. It was uncomfortable for a moment but it didn't hurt.

'You have been brought aboard our ship via our conveyor beam.' Fflqa-Tur spoke and this time I could understand every word. 'I wanted to see you for myself.'

'Well, here I am. What happens now?' I asked.

I felt so strange, so calm. For the first time, the enormity of what I was doing struck me. I was actually doing this. And unlike in one of my stories, I wouldn't be coming back. I'd never see my mother or the *Kitabu* crew again, but they would be safe and free.

And, as consolation, I was in the middle of an adventure. This was real. Not a fantasy I'd written. Not a dream in my head. Real.

'You will fight against the champion knight of my ship,' said Fflqa-Tur.

'Are you the captain of this ship?' I asked.

'I am.'

'Then I will fight against no one but you,' I said quietly.

Fflqa-Tur stared at me. Then he started to smile. I wondered if the look on his face meant that he was impressed, although for all I knew it could have been indigestion.

'Your challenge is accepted,' said Fflqa-Tur. 'Let us go to the arena.'

'One last thing.' I swallowed hard, afraid I was pushing my luck. 'I'd like our fight relayed back to the *Kitabu*. I want my… Captain Corbin and everyone else on the *Kitabu* to see our contest.'

'Agreed,' said Fflqa-Tur. 'You will now come with me. You will be clothed as a Chamrah knight and you must select your weapon.'

The arena was a small circular pit only about five metres in diameter and filled with what felt like Earth sand, only dark green in colour. Others like Fflqa-Tur sat around the arena. Funny, but they didn't look so disgusting any more. In fact they looked noble. I supposed that, given time – and the right frame of mind – you could get used to anything.

Shouts and cheers filled the air. In walked Fflqa-Tur. He was clothed as I was, in a neck-to-toe outfit that resembled an Earth-England medieval suit of armour, but the Chamrah version was almost transparent, very light and comfortable. In his hand Fflqa-Tur had what looked like a pendulum on a stick. For my weapon, I'd chosen the closest thing to a laz-sword I could find. This one was more primitive – solid metal but with a laser-sharp edge. It wouldn't have made much difference what I'd chosen really. I had never faced a real opponent in my life. An instructor robot programmed for Je-kan-ia had been my teacher. But a robot's programming would be no match for a knight skilled in the use of Chamrah weapons.

Fflqa-Tur stepped into the arena. The crowd around us fell into an expectant silence. I looked around. Was Mother watching me now? I hoped she was. If she was, what was she thinking? I would have given anything to know. Here I stood, in the arena facing Fflqa-Tur – and even now it felt as if I was failing her. If only I'd left my Peacemaker alone – how much easier it would've been.

Fflqa-Tur raised his weapon and started moving towards me. Immediately, instinctively, I backed away, raising my sword between us. Fflqa-Tur and I circled warily around each other. My heart was about to explode from my chest. I could hear the blood roaring and rushing in my ears like a stormy sea. Fflqa-Tur lunged at me. Too terrified to even cry out, I leapt back. Staring at him, I took a deep breath, then another. Then I relaxed my grip on the sword. I'd been holding it so tightly that my fingers were turning numb.

Slowly I stood up straight. I'd made up my mind. I might lose, but Fflqa-Tur would know he'd been in a fight!

The battle between us lasted longer than I thought it would – a good 45 seconds at least. That wasn't the only surprise.

I won.

Heart pounding, head throbbing, palms sweating, I won. My first two moves stopped Fflqa-Tur's attempts to lunge at me. With my third sword stroke, I knocked his weapon out of his hand. It sailed up into the air away from us. I thrust forward until the point of my sword was against Fflqa-Tur's body. He didn't say a word. No one around us moved. The silence was deafening. I watched him, he watched me. Then I threw my sword down on the ground.

I waited anxiously, unsure what to do next.

There was a long pause. Then, without warning, Fflqa-Tur tilted his head back and laughed – or rather, he did what had to be the Chamrah equivalent. The others around the arena joined in, until the air was filled with their laughing.

'Is that it?' I asked, confused. 'What happens now?'

'Well done, little one. You have passed our test.'

'Test?'

'You accepted my challenge. You fought, but you did not kill,' said Fflqa-Tur.

'Test?' Then I realized. 'You let me win! But…but I could have killed you.' I stared at him.

Fflqa-Tur beckoned to one of his crew. The crew member left his seat and came into the arena. He picked up the weapon I had just thrown on the ground. Before I could stop him, before I could even cry out, he lunged at Fflqa-Tur. I watched, wide-eyed with horror as the sword blade passed right through Fflqa-Tur's body. The captain didn't even flinch. In fact he laughed again at the look on my face.

Then I saw what had happened. All the canals filled with grey liquid and one of Fflqa-Tur's hearts had moved out of the way of the sword. They had all shifted to be either above or below the blade.

'Every part of me has a life of its own,' explained Fflqa-Tur. 'And they could see the sword coming.'

'But I don't understand. Why this test?' I said slowly, trying to take it in.

'We Chamrah have to choose our friends carefully. We are a peaceful race. We do not want aggressors as friends. Nor do we want aggressors using our trade routes. But we do not want cowards as our friends either. You showed that you were prepared to fight for what you believed in, no matter what the outcome – but you didn't kill me. You could have done but you didn't,' said Fflqa-Tur.

'Because killing is wrong,' I said.

'Then why did you accept the challenge?' Fflqa-Tur asked.

'Because…because it seemed to me that sometimes…sometimes you have to take a stand, even if you know you're going to lose.' I frowned. 'And I couldn't let you destroy our ship and kill all those people, not when I thought I could do something about it. How could I sit back and not do something about it?'

'You are indeed very brave,' said Fflqa-Tur. 'And bravery is everything.'

Bravery… Would Mother see it that way? But then a strange thought occurred to me. By refusing to kill, but not running away, didn't Mother do exactly what I was doing now? In her own way, Mother was just as brave as Fflqa-Tur. Only I'd never realized it before.

'Can they still see me on the *Kitabu*?' I asked.

'Yes.'

I turned to the viewer. 'Mother, I need to see Doctor Bevan. I did recode my Peacemaker, but don't worry. I won't tamper with it any more.'

'Peacemaker?' said the captain.

So I explained.

Fflqa-Tur said, 'But you have proven that you do not need to wear such a device. You were prepared to fight and die for your ship and your comrades, but you weren't prepared to kill needlessly. You showed compassion. That was all we needed to see.'

I looked down at my Peacemaker… and wondered.

'I will escort you to my bridge. You will be sent back to your ship from there,' said Fflqa-Tur.

As we walked back, I turned to the captain and said, 'Fflqa-Tur, may I keep my weapon and armour? As a souvenir?'

Fflqa-Tur nodded. 'Will you be punished when you return to your ship?' he asked.

'I should think so,' I sighed. Thoughts of the essays I'd have to write and the endless lectures I'd have to listen to filled my head.

'Is there no one on your ship who will be proud of you?' asked Fflqa-Tur.

'I... I don't know.' I shrugged.

Somehow... somehow I thought that Mother would understand. But even if she didn't, it wouldn't matter.

'I'm proud of myself,' I said at last. 'And that's enough.'

What was Fflqa-Tur's test?

How did Michela prove her bravery?

# One Is One and All Alone

*Nicholas Fisk*

Dear Diary,
I get so lonely, that's my trouble. I am the only child on this ship. Everyone else is a grown-up, with things to do. They're all busy running the ship or checking their equipment for when we land on the planet Trion.

Yes, we're heading for Trion! Now that might sound exciting, but it's not. It's not exciting at all.

When we set out, I used to tick off the days on my calendar. We left Earth on 12 March 2045. So I ticked off March 12, 13, 14, 15... Then April, May, June. Then I gave up. We don't reach Trion until mid-January 2047. By then I'll be 13!

Dad does his best, he's always poking his head round my door, grinning at me and asking, 'Hey Trish, how's things? Everything all right? How do you fancy meeting me in the diner at 6 o'clock for a chocolate milkshake?'

I grin back and say, 'Yum, yum!' but even as I say it his face changes. The grin is still there but the busy look is back in his eyes. There are a thousand things on his mind. After all, he's the ship's Executive Officer, a big man. Even when he talks to you he's glancing sideways at the latest printouts.

And I suppose he misses Mum as much as I do. Almost as much, anyhow. She's on Trion, helping set up the space station. Busy Dad, busy Mum.

Which leaves me all alone in front of my VoicePrinter, talking to it, talking and talking. Then I watch it print out what I've been saying. It's my private diary. It corrects my spelling and punctuation. It's clever. It gives me school lessons, but it also plays games with me. My favourite game is Pop Star, where I can act out being a pop star on VP's enormous screen.

I can switch it from Diary to Dialogue too. I suppose it's my best friend, really. I'm going to switch from Diary to Dialogue now...

ARE YOU MY BEST FRIEND, VP?

**I HOPE I AM, I TRY TO BE. BUT LATER, ON TRION, YOU WILL MEET HUMAN COMPANIONS: BOYS AND GIRLS LIKE YOURSELF.**

NOT FOR A LONG TIME, VP.

**WE MUST BE PATIENT. FOR NOW, I AM YOUR TRUE FRIEND. SHALL WE PLAY A GAME? POP STAR! SHALL WE PLAY THAT?**

OK, VP. GIVE ME A HEAVY DRUM ROLL, THEN SOME CLOUDS OF COLOURED SMOKE SO THAT I CAN MAKE MY ENTRANCE. I'D LIKE A BIG SWINGING CHAIN ROUND MY NECK.

**THIS OK?**

GREAT. RIGHT, HERE I COME, THROUGH THE SMOKE…TWO, THREE, FOUR – ACTION…

All this might sound exciting, but it's not. I'm sick of Me. I'm sick of being the only child on the ship. I'm sick of computer images and sounds. If only I had someone to talk to, to be with! Someone of my own age…

YOU KNOW WHAT I MEAN. DON'T YOU, VP?

OF COURSE I DO. I SYMPATHIZE. SHALL WE PLAY SOMETHING ELSE?

NO, LET'S NOT PLAY ANY MORE. TEACH ME SOMETHING. WHERE DID WE GET TO IN THE LAST DICTIONARY LESSON?

WE REACHED 'CLO'. SO I TAUGHT YOU ABOUT CLOCKS.

WHAT FOLLOWS 'CLOCKS'?

CLONE. C-L-O-N-E. CLONES AND CLONING.

TEACH ME ABOUT CLONES AND CLONING, THEN.

CERTAINLY. A CLONE IS THE EXACT REPRODUCTION OF A LIVING THING, MADE

BY TAKING A SMALL PART OF THE ORIGINAL – SAY A SCRAP OF TISSUE – AND USING THIS SCRAP AS THE PATTERN FROM WHICH A DUPLICATE OF THE ORIGINAL IS CREATED.

OH DEAR! THAT SOUNDS VERY COMPLICATED. NO, WAIT, I REMEMBER NOW. THEY CLONED SHEEP IN THE LAST CENTURY, DIDN'T THEY?

**SHEEP AND MANY OTHER ANIMALS.**

THAT'S RIGHT. THEY TOOK A TINY SCRAPING FROM THE SHEEP'S SKIN AND SORT OF BREWED UP HUNDREDS OF SHEEP FROM THAT LITTLE SCRAPING.

**QUITE SO. AND ALL THE SHEEP WERE IDENTICAL BECAUSE ALL WERE CONSTRUCTED FROM THE SAME ORIGINAL AND TO THE SAME PATTERN.**

I BET IT WAS COMPLICATED!

**IT WAS. IT IS.**

YOU MEAN, IT'S STILL DONE?

CERTAINLY. WHY, THE RESOURCES
AVAILABLE IN THIS SHIP'S BIOLAB WOULD
BE SUFFICIENT TO SET UP A CLONE
LABORATORY. YOU SEE, ALL THAT IS
REQUIRED...

VP went on and on describing cloning techniques so I decided to press 'Save' and listen to it all later. For now I had some serious thinking to do.

I'll tell you what I was thinking. The BioLab in this ship is very big. It has to be, because biology is what this trip is all about – the biology of Trion – what lives there now and what, and who, could live there in the future. At the moment the ship's BioLab is deserted. It won't become busy until we reach Trion.

I need to use it.

I need it all to myself.

I will make a clone. It will be my perfect friend and companion. Perfect, because I am going to clone myself. Make another Me.

Dear Diary,

I haven't spoken to you for ages because I've been so busy with my new friend Clo.

Clo for 'Clone'.

Clo is me. I am Clo. We are identical twins. No, even closer than that. Clo is made of me, from me. We are one. Except that there are two of us – which is tricky. I mean, suppose Dad put his head round the door and saw two Trishes instead of one!

But I've solved that. My cabin door leads to an identical cabin next door. Clo can vanish through that door in a split second. The next-door cabin is empty, of course – all the cabins are. They won't be filled until the return trip from Trion. So I sleep here, Clo sleeps there. Clothes, food, toothbrushes? Well, yes, I now need two of everything – but the ship is loaded with stores. Nobody notices or cares about an extra toothbrush or an extra towel.

In fact, everything's fine as long as we don't both appear in the same place at the same time! We simply arrange not to. Though, just the other night, we nearly made a big mistake...

In the middle of the night I had to go to the loo. It's just down the corridor. I got out of bed, opened the door – and met myself, face to face! For there was Clo. We stared at each other, eyes and mouths wide open, then burst into identical giggles.

Which all goes to show how identical we are. We even go to the loo at the same time!

No wonder we're such perfect friends.

Dear Diary,

Once again, it's been a long time since I spoke to you. There have been so many things on my mind. The truth is, Clo can be a bit of a pain sometimes. Only in small ways, nothing serious. But she has this picking habit. When Clo has nothing to do, it's always pick, pick, pick. Rolling bits of skin around a fingernail. You can't avoid looking at her fingers. They writhe and fiddle all the time. Pick, pick, pick.

The other evening, I'd had enough. I gave Clo a good old glare and said, loudly and plainly, 'Look – do you mind? Stop picking at yourself!'

You'll never believe it, but at the very moment I said those words, Clo glared at me and said, 'Look – do you mind? Stop picking at yourself!'

*Me*, a picker! I never pick at my fingers. Those tiny little bits of frayed skin – well, they just happen naturally. Everyone's got them.

I can't stand people who pick.


Dear Diary,
Hello again my dear old VP, my only true friend.

Clo is in the other cabin, having a sulk. She always sulks these days and it always starts the same way...

'Don't keep repeating me!'

'I wasn't repeating you, I spoke first!'

'You didn't. I did.'

'Well, even if I didn't say it first, I thought it first. I can't even have my thoughts to myself, you're always butting in and – and – interrupting my train of thought!'

'Interrupting my train of thought.'

We even use the same words at the same time.

At first it was a joke. We'd catch ourselves doing it and laugh. But I'm not laughing any more, I can tell you. I don't want to share everything: some thoughts are private.

Last night Clo did something I cannot forgive. I was thinking about Mum – I'm always thinking of her – and I suppose I gave a sort of sigh and murmured, 'Oh, Mum...'

As I said it, Clo said precisely the same thing. 'Oh, Mum...' Clo said, and gave a sigh.

Now, that's going too far, don't you agree? I mean, my mum is my mum, nothing to do with Clo. My mum, mine only.

I'm not going to put up with this kind of thing. It's like being swamped, invaded, taken over. She wears the same clothes as me. And crossword puzzles! Well, how would you like it when, after puzzling over a clue for ages, you suddenly find the answer and shout it out – 'NAVIGATOR!' – and, at that very moment, hear a voice from the cabin next door shout 'NAVIGATOR!'

And those are only the small things. To be truthful, I can't stand the way Clo's mind works. I can't stand Clo's corny jokes, and her dismal sulks. I can't stand Clo's laugh or eating habits or finger-picking. And I won't stand Clo intruding on my most private and personal thoughts.

One of the features of this ship is its disposal system. There are five big hatches, each one marked 'DISPOSAL'. You open the hatch, put the thing you want to get rid of into the hole, and whoosh, it's gone. Disposed of for ever in infinite space.

One of the five hatches happens to be just outside my cabin, in the corridor. There's never anyone in the corridor at night.

There you are, then. Tonight's the night. I'll be disposing of something, definitely. I'm going to write a note to go with the item. The note will read, 'Goodbye, Clo. Have a good trip. Yours never, Trish.'

Well, it wouldn't be murder, would it? How could it be? You can't be charged with murdering yourself, can you? You couldn't even be charged with suicide, because there will still be a person left and that person will be alive – walking and talking, eating and sleeping.

So it's foolproof. 'Goodbye, Clo. Yours never, Trish.'

Dear Diary,
Over and done with. Finished and forgotten.

No, that's not true! There's no question of forgetting. Just the opposite. Every minute of every hour, I mentally hug myself and give a silent shout of 'Whoopee! Yarroop! Hooray! Finally free! Alone at last!'

Even Dad noticed a change in me. 'You're looking wonderful today,' he said. 'Suddenly you're bright as a button!'

'I feel terrific,' I said. 'Can I have a chocolate milkshake?'

'Have as many as you like.'

'Just one,' I said. 'Only one. One's enough, isn't it? Who needs two?' There's only one Me! No longer do I have to remind another Me to wipe chocolate froth from its greedy mouth. No longer do I have to listen to that other Me's corny 'Yum-yum!' noises whenever chocolate milkshakes are mentioned. From now on, there's only one Me. You've no idea how wonderful it feels, how bright the future looks.

Too bad about Trish, of course. 'Down the hatch!' I said. The hatch went whoosh. 'Goodbye, Trish,' I said. 'Happy memories, I don't think.'

But that's something I must remember from now on – my name. It isn't Clo any more. Now I'm Trish.

Trish, that's me.

What would be the advantages and disadvantages of having a clone?

# Rehearsal

*David Belbin*

'Life's not a rehearsal. You only get one chance,' Joel's parents said after they had returned from the parents' evening at his school. 'You must try harder.'

'I will, I promise,' said Joel, then hurried off to play with his computer. He was up to the fourth level of his new game Robo-riot.

Joel's teacher, Miss Mulch, had told his mum and dad that Joel would not do well in his end of year tests. 'Not unless he does a lot more work,' she warned.

But Joel didn't really care what Miss Mulch, or his parents, said about his school work. He was more interested in getting to the fifth and final level of Robo-riot.

'Joel! What do you think you're doing?' his mum said, coming in hours after Joel had pretended to go to bed. 'It's nearly midnight!' She unplugged the computer just as the riot was about to begin. Joel was furious.

Next day at school, Joel was tired and irritable. Miss Mulch told him off for copying his history project from Darren, his best friend. Why should she care? Darren didn't mind.

When Joel got home that evening, there was something strange in the hall. It was tall and metallic, like a hi-tech telephone kiosk. It had its own generator on the side.

'What's going on?' he asked, as the shiny machine began to shimmer and vibrate.

'It's a prototype from your father's factory. He's testing it out to make sure that it's safe,' Mum said.

'But what is it?' Joel asked.

'It's a virtual future machine.'

'Sounds daft,' Joel said. 'No one can see into the future.'

'It's not the real future,' Mum explained, 'more a kind of prediction. You have to sit inside the machine, hook the leads up to your head and tell the machine where you want to go in your life. Then you find out what happens. It's supposed to be like a very realistic dream. But we don't know how well it works yet.'

The machine stopped vibrating and the door opened. Dad came out, looking excited.

'It's great,' he said. 'In two years' time I'll set up my own company manufacturing mini virtual future machines and make a fortune.'

'Can I have a go?' Joel pleaded.

'After dinner,' Mum said.

'How does the machine work?' Joel asked as they ate.

Dad explained. 'You put on a headset which reads your personality and your past actions. Then you have to think hard and decide what course to take in life. The machine reads your thoughts and shows you how things might work out.'

'Perhaps you'll learn something from it,' Mum said.

'I can't wait!' Joel exclaimed.

As soon as he had finished his food, Joel jumped up from the table and ran over to the machine.

'Don't stay in for more than half an hour,' Dad warned, 'or you might get a headache.'

Inside the machine, Joel found himself surrounded by reflective screens. It was like being in a three-dimensional photo booth. There was a joystick, so you could go forwards or backwards, and an on/off switch. Joel pressed it. At first, he thought the machine wasn't going to work. It whirred but nothing happened. Then Joel gave the joystick a thrust and whoosh! His life rushed forward – school, home, computer, sleep. It was fascinating and funny, too, how the days all looked the same.

Joel slowed down when he reached the next school sports afternoon. He was last up to bat and his cricket team had a terrible score. Joel concentrated. He batted cautiously but well. Modestly, he declared at 20 runs and fast forwarded to the fielding, where he made two catches. In the end his team won and everyone said that the result was down to him. It was a great feeling.

Joel pressed the on/off switch and stepped out of the machine. Excitedly, he told his mum and dad how well he'd done.

'Next time,' Mum suggested, 'see what happens if you study hard.'

Joel's mum and dad had entered him for the scholarship exam to go to St Theodore's, the poshest school in the county. But Joel hadn't been revising. He'd probably left it too late. So, after school the next day, Joel used the virtual future machine again. Perhaps he could find out what would happen in the exam.

He was getting the hang of it now, nudging the joystick gently. Joel studied every night for the next three weeks, until the day of the exam. The questions were a breeze. To be sure of the result, Joel fast forwarded a whole month, to when the letter from St Theodore's arrived. He'd passed!

'I hope you'll start revising for the real exam now,' Mum said, when Joel told them about the machine's prediction.

'You bet!' said Joel. 'But can I have another go in the machine tonight? Can I, please? Just a short one.'

His parents agreed.

This time Joel tried to fast forward to his new life at St Theodore's, but he didn't concentrate as hard as he had earlier. This time, when the exam results came, he hadn't passed. Joel fast forwarded a bit more. Disappointed by his failure, Joel did not try very hard at the local school he went to instead of St Theodore's. He began to muck about. Soon he took up smoking and started skiving off school. The only thing he really tried hard at was sport. But then, just as he was about to captain the school football team, Joel found himself being expelled. He had been caught stealing money from another boy's bag.

Joel switched the machine off.

'Joel, it's after midnight. What were you doing in there all this time?' Dad said.

'Learning the hard way,' Joel said.

'Do you feel all right?' Dad asked. 'I was worried that you had been in there for too long, but couldn't reach in and turn the machine off. You see, the inventor warned me that it could be very dangerous to interrupt someone using the machine.'

'I'm fine,' Joel said. 'No headache. I'm quite hungry though.'

'Get some supper. And from now on, promise, only half an hour at the most.'

Joel promised. For the next two nights, he studied hard and only had short sessions in the machine. As a result, he never got further than a year or so into the future. Each time Joel made sure that he got into St Theodore's. But he didn't enjoy it much. There were too many rules and the teachers were terribly strict. Joel couldn't imagine staying there for seven years. He wondered what would happen if he tried a different route.

At the weekend, Joel went round to Darren's house. He'd been warned not to tell anyone about the machine as Dad had signed a secrecy agreement, but he couldn't resist making hints.

'What would you do if you could travel into the future and be anything you wanted?' he asked his friend.

'A big pop star,' Darren said.

'No use,' Joel said. 'I can't sing like you can.'

'I know,' said Darren. 'You could be a footballer.'

'I'm better at cricket,' said Joel.

'Yeah, but cricketers don't earn anywhere near as much money,' Darren pointed out.

That night, Joel crept out of his room after his mum and dad had gone to bed and climbed into the machine. He knew it would take more than half an hour to learn how to become a famous footballer.

On this trip, Joel forgot about going to St Theodore's and, instead, practised football at every opportunity. Soon, he got a place in the local school's team. At first, he was selfish with the ball. He scored goals but wasn't popular with the other players. So he rewound a few weeks and became more generous. By the end of his first year, Joel was team captain.

He fast forwarded, concentrating hard. At the age of 15, Joel was good enough to have trials for Manchester United and Liverpool. Unfortunately, he was only offered a place in the local club's youth team. Joel rewound and tried to play better. This time, he got an offer from Chelsea, so he left school and joined the club to play for the reserves.

On Joel's 18th birthday, the manager told him that he was letting him go.

'You're an intelligent player, a good athlete. But I don't think you've got what it takes to make it in the Premier League. I'm sure you can have a career in one of the lower divisions.'

But only big success would satisfy Joel. He wasn't going to give up now. He rewound all the way back to the exam. He passed it. This time, he concentrated on playing cricket for St Theodore's. After all, he was better at cricket than football. Joel learned to bat better and be more disciplined about his fielding. He did well, but there were lots of other cricketers in the school and it took him a while to make his mark. Eventually, however, he became school captain, and not long after that he made it into the Lancashire team. Once he'd rewound and fast forwarded for the twentieth or thirtieth time, Joel got to play for England – twice!

After that, life was an anti-climax. Joel got married and had a family. He opened a sports shop which was a big success. But nothing excited him like playing cricket for England. As he fast forwarded through the life he would have, Joel realized that he had made the wrong choice. A career in sport was usually over by the time you were 30. But what could he do instead? He would have to think about that.

Joel switched off the machine, took off the headset and tried to get out. There was something attached to his arm. It was a kind of tube. Joel shrieked. His mum and dad came running downstairs. He'd woken them up.

Joel expected them both to be angry with him, but his mum just burst into tears. 'Thank God you're all right!' she said.

'What's this thing on my arm?' Joel asked.

'It's a drip feed,' Dad told him. 'You've been inside the machine for four days! We were worried that you might starve to death so we called a doctor. She said that switching off the machine might kill you and suggested the drip.'

Joel couldn't believe how long he'd been gone.

'Look at yourself in the mirror,' Mum said.

Joel was pale and pasty faced.

'I'm sorry,' he told his parents. 'I got carried away. But I played cricket for England!'

In a rush, he told them all that he'd been through.

'That's all very well,' Dad said, 'but, first thing tomorrow, the machine goes back!'

'I haven't worked out what I want to do with my life yet!'

'If you pass your exam and go to St Theodore's,' said Dad, 'you'll have plenty of time to work out the next part. But you've lost four days' studying. You must be exhausted, young man. Come on, off to bed.'

Joel went to bed, but he wasn't tired. It was as though all he'd done for the last four days was sleep. His mind went into overdrive. He'd seen the next few years so many times. Apart from the odd sporting success, they were really boring. If Joel was going to go through them again, he had to be sure that there was something brilliant waiting at the end. But the machine was going back to the factory in the morning. What could he do?

Joel had no choice. He had to have one more go on the machine. He listened carefully to make sure that his mum and dad had gone back to sleep, then sneaked downstairs. He wrote a note saying 'Sorry, I might be gone for some time', stuck it on the door of the machine and went in.

Joel knew that his mum and dad would feed him while he was inside. So now he could stay for as long as he needed. He would rehearse his life until he'd worked out exactly what to do with it.

This time Joel was a good student at St Theodore's. He kept his head down and tried to be popular with everyone. After that, he went to university and studied law. He met a girl called Gemma. They got married and moved to London where they worked as barristers and made lots of money. They worked hard and went on expensive holidays, had a nanny for the children, and drove big, fast cars.

When Joel hit 30, he slowed down to take a closer look at a typical evening. It was quiet. The kids had gone to bed and Gemma was working late. Joel switched on the television and flicked through the channels.

This life was boring. Would life be more exciting if he was an actor? How about a politician? They seemed to have lots of power. Or there was the army. The world never seemed to run out of wars.

He put on a music channel, remembering Darren's suggestion that he should become a pop star. A guitarist was playing a brilliant solo. Why not? Joel thought.

Whoosh! He left his comfortable but boring life behind and went right back to the day after tomorrow.

'Not studying today?' Darren asked, as they walked home from school.

'I decided to forget St Theodore's,' Joel told him. 'I want to learn to play the guitar.'

'Cool!' Darren said. 'Want to have a go on mine?'

Joel couldn't sing, but proved to be talented on guitar. When they were 13, he and Darren formed a group. It took a few rewinds, but by the time they were 16 the group had a recording contract. They left school and began to tour the world. It was a bit of a drag, actually, all that travelling and living in hotels. But the concerts were great.

There was just one problem. Darren was better at music than Joel. No matter how often Joel rewound and tried again, a moment always came where Darren left the group and went solo. Darren became an even bigger success but Joel's career faded. At 30, Joel was more washed up than he'd been as a cricketer. Maybe a lawyer's life wasn't so bad after all.

Joel rewound and tried a different tack. Again he went to St Theodore's and did well. This time, though, he joined the school debating society. At university, he got to be Union President. He became a barrister, then an MP. At 44, after endless rewinds to avoid mistakes, he became Prime Minister.

But, being the most powerful person in the country, Joel soon discovered, was very lonely. It was exciting at times, but the boring bits outnumbered them ten to one. And it was such hard work.

One day, when visiting his parents, Joel bumped into Darren. Without Joel to push him, Darren hadn't become a rock star. Instead he had a small business making toys. Darren pretended to be impressed by Joel's position, but Joel could tell that he wasn't, not really.

'You always wanted to be a big success,' Darren said. 'Now you are.'

Returning home to Downing Street, Joel felt empty and tired. There was no need to fast forward into the future. The rehearsal, he decided, was over. He had learned what he could do, if he tried hard, and if he was very lucky. But maybe the best bits of life couldn't be planned for any more than the boring bits could be missed out. If you always wanted more, Joel had decided, you would never be satisfied.

Perhaps he should just go back, get out of the machine, and get on with his real life. He hoped that he hadn't missed his exam.

Joel pressed the off button. Then he took off his headset, unplugged his drip and, unsteady on his feet, half fell out of the machine.

Home didn't look like home any more. It looked like a hospital. Had he been ill? Joel shivered. His dressing gown didn't seem to be keeping him warm.

'Mum!' he yelled. 'Dad?' His voice sounded strangely deep. A young nurse appeared in the corridor.

'Who are you?' she said.

'I'm Joel,' he told her. 'I've just come out of that machine.'

'Oh. It's because of you they banned those machines,' the nurse said.

'They've banned them?' Joel asked.

'Yes. It's a pity. I really wanted a go in one when I was a kid.'

'But they didn't have them then,' Joel said.

The nurse gave him a funny look.

A really old couple were coming down the corridor. The man was in a zimmer frame. The woman managed with just a stick.

'It's him!' the woman said, as they got closer. 'It's Joel!'

To his horror, Joel recognized his mum's voice.

'Where am I?' he said.

'You're in an old people's home,' Dad told him. 'They moved the machine here so you could be near us.'

'I must be dreaming,' Joel said. 'I've been in the machine for a few days, that's all.'

'You lost track of time,' Mum told him. 'You were gone for years.'

'How many years?' Joel asked, as the truth began to sink in.

'Too many,' Dad said. 'Look in the mirror.'

Joel saw a pasty-faced old man with a long wispy beard, his body only half-covered by a child's dressing gown.

'You've been gone for fifty-five years,' said Mum.

In horror, Joel backed away from his parents. He looked at himself in the mirror once more, then, before anyone could do anything, jumped back into the machine and pressed the on switch.

'It's no good,' Mum called out, as Joel reached for the joystick.

She was right, Joel realized, for he

couldn't go back in his real life like he could in his virtual future life. As he pressed the joystick, the days passed by in a blur, every one of them the same. He was a 66-year-old man, with little future and even less past. His whole life had been a wasted rehearsal.

Do you think it would be a good thing if you could design your own future?

# Trust Me

*Tony Bradman*

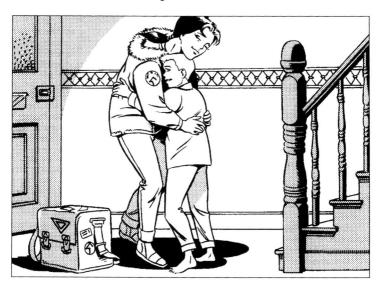

Scott had been trying to get to sleep for ages when he heard a car stop in the quiet street outside. He lay rigid and listened to muffled voices, the car moving off, footsteps coming up the path, the sound of a key in the front door. By the time the door was fully open, he was half-way down the stairs. Mum put her bag on the floor carefully, and held her arms wide.

'Now that's what I call a welcome,' she said as Scott hugged her, his cheek pressed against the cold nylon of her parka. He looked up at her face. Mum gave him one of those 'Everything's-Going-To-Be-All-Right' smiles of hers. But Scott knew she was just as worried as he was. How could it be otherwise with Dad in hospital, fighting for his life?

'We weren't expecting you until tomorrow,' Scott said, letting Mum go at last and standing back. After three months of only seeing her once a week on a computer monitor, he could hardly believe she was really here, and not still in Antarctica. 'I thought you told Gran on the phone there was something you had to take to the lab before you could come home.'

'I just decided I was totally desperate to see my favourite ten year old tear-away first,' said Mum, and kissed him. 'So... here I am. You'd better wake your gran.'

A few moments later, Scott led a bleary-eyed Gran into the kitchen, just as Mum took a lunchbox-sized silver case from her bag, and placed it in the fridge. Scott recognized it immediately. It was her container for the biological samples she collected in her work as a research scientist.

Mum shut the fridge and hugged Gran, and they sat down with mugs of tea. Scott wondered when Mum would notice the state of the pot plant on the table, but she paid it no attention. She just wanted to hear about Dad.

Scott stayed silent as Gran filled in the details of what had happened since the car crash, nearly a week ago, and what Dad's doctor had told them today. Scott's eyes drifted to the withered plant, and he felt a surge of guilt. He remembered again what Mum had said on the day she'd left.

'Scott, here are your instructions,' she'd said with a smile. 'You're a big boy now, so you're in charge of feeding the cat, watering my pot plants, and making sure Dad looks after himself. Can I trust you to do all that?'

'Sure, Mum,' he'd said, not paying any attention.

Mum was always going on about trust and being able to rely on people, but Scott rarely took any notice. Which is why Shackleton, their ginger tom, would probably have starved to death if it hadn't been for Dad. And also why most of Mum's plants were looking pretty sickly. But since the accident, Scott had found himself thinking about Mum's words a lot.

He kept thinking that he'd let her down – especially as he had pestered Dad for a lift home from school that day, when he could easily have walked home.

'So what are you going to do?' Gran was asking.

'I'm going to the hospital, of course,' said Mum, and finished her tea. 'I asked the cab driver to give me half an hour, then to come back. I wanted to see Scott and you, find out what's been happening, and get my samples in the fridge. If they're not at the lab, they need to be kept safe, at least.'

'Why?' said Gran, slightly puzzled. 'Are they important?'

'Oh yes,' said Mum. 'In fact, they could be the most important scientific discovery ever. We think they might be live bacteria …from outer space.'

'You're kidding!' said Scott, suddenly interested, despite his worries.

'No, I'm not,' said Mum. 'We found them on a meteorite we dug up ten days ago, and they're like nothing we've encountered before. I was starting to test them when I heard about your dad. I had to come home, so the director gave me clearance to bring some of the samples back for evaluation at the lab.'

'Er, you don't think I could…' Scott said.

'Take a look at them?' said Mum, wearily. 'Absolutely not, Scott. You know the rule…my samples are strictly off-limits. We've got enough problems without you letting loose some strange alien disease that might annihilate the human race. I know it's tempting, but try and be responsible for once, OK? You needn't think I haven't noticed the plants, by the way.'

71

'I'm sorry, Mum,' Scott mumbled. He could feel himself blushing. 'And I'm sorry, too,' said Mum, hugging him tight again. 'I didn't mean to be grumpy with you. I'm just a bit tired from the flight, that's all.'

'I can hear a car,' said Gran. 'It must be your cab.'

'I'm coming with you,' said Scott as Mum rose from her chair.

'I really don't think that's a good idea, Scott,' said Gran gently, exchanging meaningful looks with Mum. 'You were at the hospital the whole day, and you need some rest. We'd best let your mum go alone.'

'Your gran's right,' said Mum quickly before Scott could protest. One look at her face told him there was no point in arguing. 'Don't worry though, sweetheart,' she added. 'I'll be sure to give Dad your love.'

But there was no 'Everything's-Going-To-Be-All-Right' smile this time.

Scott and Gran waved goodbye to Mum from the front door, then went back to bed. Scott lay rigid under his duvet in the midnight quiet, his mind racing, and he soon realized sleep was more unlikely than ever.

He got out of bed, crept downstairs, and went into the kitchen. It was dark in there now, although there was enough pale star-glow coming through the window for him to see Mum's and Gran's mugs on the table.

Scott suddenly felt thirsty and opened the fridge. Bright white light spilled around him as he reached in for a carton of orange juice. But there was something in front of the juice – Mum's container for biological samples.

Scott had no choice but to remove the container. He carefully placed it on the table, next to the pot holding the withered plant. Then he pulled out the carton of orange juice, took a tall glass from a cupboard, and poured himself a drink.

He sipped and stared at the container. It shone with a dull gleam in the star-glow from the window, looking more like lead than silver. Scott could hardly believe what Mum had said. Under normal circumstances, it would be incredible to think he was close to something that might be alien.

But the only thing that mattered in the universe right now was Dad.

Scott sighed. He felt utterly useless, as

well as guilty. It had been awful at the hospital today, seeing Dad wired up to those bleeping machines, knowing that the hushed voice of the doctor and the sad looks he'd got from the nurses meant things were bad for Dad, very bad indeed. If only there was something he could do, thought Scott. But he was just a kid...

There was nothing for it. He would have to go to bed, and keep waiting and worrying. He reached for the container to put it away, then stopped. The small, numbered key pad and display on one side had caught his eye.

Scott knew it was for entering a code that would unlock the container. He remembered a similar keypad on a container of samples Mum had brought home once before. Mum didn't know that Scott had cracked her code in about two seconds. She had used the dates of their three birthdays – 15, 22, 27. Scott thought about Dad's birthday earlier this year, and wondered if Dad would live to add another digit to his age. And while his mind was mostly distracted, his fingers idly tapped in the code numbers, as if by habit.

'Oh, no...' Scott said, suddenly

realizing what he'd done.

The numbers flashed up on the display, there was a click, and the case opened. Both sides moved outwards until they formed a stand for a metal frame, the whole thing ending up slightly taller than the pot plant beside it. The frame contained two glass tubes, one larger than the other. Both contained liquid, and both were giving off a faint, spooky, bluish glow.

Scott knew from what Mum had told him that the liquid was water, with the bacteria suspended in it. But he'd never seen any samples like these. They really did look, well…alien was the only word for it.

Scott couldn't help being fascinated with

what was in the case, but then he started to feel guilty again. Mum would definitely not be pleased with him if she knew what he was doing at that moment. He really ought to close the case and put it away. But he didn't get the chance.

Suddenly there was a thumping at the back door that made Scott jump. Then he realized it was only Shackleton, clumsily pushing through his cat flap. The ginger cat came trotting straight over to Scott, miaowing loudly.

'OK, keep your fur on,' murmured Scott, thinking he might as well do one of the things Mum had entrusted him with. 'I know what you want.'

Scott stood up and went over to the cupboard for a tin of cat food. He got the opener out of the cutlery drawer and started opening the tin.

But Scott was tired, and he hadn't put the light on, and his hand slipped. Scott sensed a sharp pain in his finger as the tin skated away from him and fell to the floor. Shackleton leapt in fright and shot off under the table, bumping against a leg. Scott watched in horror as the container toppled on to the plant – and the smaller tube cracked on the edge of the pot.

The bluish liquid immediately drained into the compost. Scott dashed across the kitchen and desperately stood the container up – but it was too late. The tube was completely empty now. Just then, Scott realized another liquid was dripping off the end of his finger and into the case. He looked and saw he had quite a nasty cut that was bleeding steadily.

Scott's heart sunk. Even though he hadn't meant to, he'd done the worst thing imaginable. He had really let his mum down now. He had lost some of the most precious samples in the history of science, and because of him she would probably get into serious trouble. Then he remembered what she had said about strange alien diseases annihilating the human race…

Then the most amazing thing happened, and Scott's jaw dropped with surprise. The plant on the table began to glow, with the same blue glow as the test tubes, but now it was pulsing through the plant's stem and leaves. And as Scott watched, the plant seemed to grow healthy again, until finally, when the blue glow faded, it stood there in its pot looking perfect.

Scott closed his mouth and noticed there was a tiny globule of the blue liquid hanging on the rim of the pot. He glanced at his finger, then held it under the droplet, which obligingly fell on to his cut. The tip of his finger immediately began to glow, his hand tingled…and the cut simply knitted itself together. When the glow faded, his finger was as good as new.

One thought instantly filled Scott's mind. If a tiny amount of the alien bacteria could heal a cut just like that – what might a large amount do for Dad? Scott picked up the bigger tube, and weighed it in his hand. His excitement grew, then collapsed again like a punctured balloon. How would he explain it to Mum? She'd probably just get cross and not listen.

Now Scott's mind became crowded with worries. The alien bacteria hadn't been tested, he might start turning into an alien monster any second, using them on Dad might not work, Mum would get into serious trouble...and it would all be Scott's fault. He would be letting Mum down, yet again.

But that was a risk he would have to take, he decided. Time was running out for Dad and Scott knew the bacteria were his only chance. Suddenly Scott's mind was clear and he knew exactly what to do.

'Gran!' he yelled, running upstairs. 'We have to get a cab...now!'

Half an hour later, Scott left an even more bleary-eyed, cross and dazed Gran paying a cab driver and ran into the hospital. He dashed to Intensive Care, pushed open the door, and walked swiftly towards the familiar bed.

Dad was still there, still wired up to the bleeping machines, and Mum was sitting next to him, holding his hand, her head bowed. She looked up as Scott approached, and he could see she had been crying.

'I just couldn't stay at home, Mum,' he said, 'so I've come to give you a break.

Gran's downstairs in the cafe, getting you a cup of tea.'

'I could certainly do with one,' said Mum. 'But I'm not sure I ought to leave you here on your own. You're not to get up to any mischief now…'

'Don't worry, Mum,' said Scott, giving her an 'Everything-Will-Be-All-Right-Smile' of his own, and touching the tube in his pocket. 'Trust me.'

What would you do if you had a small amount of the healing bacteria?